Violins

Music Makers

THE CHILD'S WORLD®, INC.

Violins

Pamela K. Harris

THE CHILD'S WORLD®, INC.

Library of Congress Cataloging-in-Publication Data
Harris, Pamela K., 1962–
Violins / by Pamela K. Harris.
 p. cm.
Summary: Simple text describes violins, how they are made, and how they are played.
ISBN 1-56766-681-7 (lib. bdg. : alk. paper)
1. Violin—Juvenile literature. [1. Violin.]
ML800 .H18 2000
787.2'19—dc21   99-059949

Credits

Translation: Neil Carruthers,
University of Canterbury, Christchurch, New Zealand
Graphic design: Brad Clemmons

Photo Credits

© www.comstock.com: 20
© Corbis Images: 6
© PhotoDisc: 19, 23
© Stone/Howard Kingsnorth: cover, 3, back cover;
  Bob Torrez: 9; David Ash: 10; Mary Kate Denny: 13;
  Terry Vine: 15; Mitch York: 16

Table of Contents

If you look closely at a violin, you can see that it looks like a big, fancy "*8*." The body of the violin is called the **soundbox.** The soundbox has two holes in it that look like the letter "*f*." The handle on the violin is called the **neck.**

The violin belongs to a group of musical instruments called **stringed instruments.** Guitars and banjos are stringed instruments, too.

← The shape of a violin is like the number "*8*."

Who Makes Violins?

Instead of being made by machines, violins are made by people. These violin makers are called **luthiers.** Luthiers go to special schools to learn how to make violins. They must practice for many years before they become good violin makers.

This luthier is proud of the violin she has made. →

What Are Violins Made Of?

Violins are made of wood. There are many pieces of wood in a violin—more than 70! The wood comes from spruce and maple trees. Violins made from spruce trees sound different from violins made from maple trees.

To make a violin, a tree is cut into slices. Then the slices are set out to dry for at least ten years. After drying, the wood is shaped to create the violin's soundbox and neck. Look closely at the violin's wood. You can see tiny waves in it. These waves help to carry the sound the violin makes.

How Do You Play a Violin?

A violin has strings like a guitar. You can play a violin like a guitar by plucking its strings. But most of the time, you use a **bow** to play it. A bow is a long rod strung with horsehair. You rub the bow back and forth over the strings. This causes the strings to **vibrate,** or move back and forth. The vibrating strings make the sounds, or **notes,** that you hear.

The sound of a violin can make people happy. ➔

The Strings

A violin has only four strings. How can you use it to play more than four notes? To do this, you need to know some things about the strings of instruments. The length of the strings changes the notes the instrument makes. Long strings make low notes, and short strings make high notes.

These violinists are part of an orchestra. →

On a violin, all the strings are the same length. How do you make them shorter? By pressing each string against the violin's neck, you change how long the string is. It's almost as if you were cutting the string! But you can make the string long again by taking your finger off it.

Can you see another difference between the strings? Some strings are thicker than others. The thickness of each string also changes how the notes sound. Thick strings play low notes. Thin strings play high notes.

The Bridge

Do you see the little piece of wood under the strings? It is called the **bridge.** The bridge helps hold the strings up off the violin's soundbox. This makes it easier for the strings to vibrate.

You can see how this violin's bridge is holding up the strings. →

19

Before you can play a violin, you must do one more thing. You must make sure that all the strings are stretched to just the right tightness. You do this by twisting the little knobs at the end of the violin's neck. As you stretch the strings, they vibrate more quickly and sound higher. This is called **tuning** the violin.

← The tuning pegs on a violin help keep the strings tight and in tune.

Violinists also make sure their violins are "in tune" with other players' violins. This means that their strings are vibrating at the same rate. Listen before a concert and you will hear the violinists tuning their violins. It sounds very noisy! Now you are ready to play the violin!

Other Stringed Instruments

harp

string bass

viella

lute

cello

classical guitar

23

Glossary

bow (BOH)
A bow is a long rod with long hairs strung between the ends. Rubbing a bow across a violin's strings makes a sound.

bridge (BRIDJ)
A bridge is a little piece of wood on a violin that holds the strings up off the soundbox. The bridge lets the strings vibrate more easily.

luthiers (LOO-thee-erz)
A luthier is a person who makes violins by hand. People go to special schools to learn how to make violins.

neck (NEK)
The neck is the part of a violin that looks like a handle. Pressing the strings against the neck changes the strings' sounds.

notes (NOHTZ)
A note is a musical sound. The strings on a violin play different notes.

soundbox (SOUND BAHKS)
A violin's soundbox is its body. The soundbox is hollow and helps to make the music louder.

stringed instruments (STRINGD IN-struh-ments)
Stringed instruments are musical instruments that use stretched strings to make their sounds. Violins are stringed instruments.

tuning (TOO-ning)
Tuning a violin is stretching the strings to get the sound you want. The tighter the string is, the higher it sounds.

vibrate (VY-brayt)
When something vibrates, it moves back and forth. When a violin's strings vibrate, they make sounds.

Index

DRAGON SCHOOL

CAMILA

THE MIRROR LAKE

LONG

FIN OCEAN

For George and Kelsey, who inspired me
to find my own path.
—H.W.

There really *are* dragons in this world.
Stay curious then you will find them.
—M.B.

Published by Yeehoo Press
6540 Lusk Blvd, Ste C152, San Diego, CA 92121
yeehoopress.com

The illustrations for this book were created in watercolor and pencil.
Edited by Peng Shen
Designed by Si Ye
Supervised by Luyang Xue

Library of Congress Control Number: 2022931497
ISBN: 978-1-953458-50-6
Printed in China First Edition
3 4 5 6 7 8 9 10

LONG GOES TO DRAGON SCHOOL

By Helen H. Wu   Illustrated by Mae Besom

YEEHOO
PRESS

Today is the first day of Dragon School.

Long is excited about his new adventure and so are his classmates, Camila, Willy, and Mia.

"Welcome to the class! We're here to discover your unique talents," Professor McKay says. "First, we'll learn how to use our fire breath to cook food."

I've read that in a book.

Professor McKay gathers everyone
and picks up a big potato.
"Who likes roasted potatoes?"

I do!

I do!

I do!

I do!

*What can I do? I can't
roast potatoes with
water!* Long thinks.

"Now, watch closely," Professor McKay says.

"Relax your body, focus your mind,
feel your power, fire you'll find!"

FRIZZLE

FRAZZLE

FROOZZ

A bright jet of fire comes out from Professor McKay's mouth, and—just like that—the potato is fire-roasted and ready to eat.

"Now it's your turn," Professor McKay says. "When you're ready, we'll have a picnic. Everyone will join in cooking the food. It's time to practice!"

"Relax your body, focus your mind, feel your power, fire you'll find!"

Camila's face turns red.

Willy sneezes out a plume of smoke.

Mia coughs up a gob of ash.

Long huffs and puffs, but all that comes out is a shower of water. He taps his feet, thinking, *I have to look like I can breathe fire!*

Long looks around and sprinkles some dust on his nose.

"You'll find your own path," Professor McKay tells the class. "It takes time and lots of practice!"

Mia blows out flames and the potato cracks.

Camila spews lava and the potato turns to ash.

Willy burps fire and the potato melts.

Long only gushes out a spray of warm water.

He fidgets and grabs some dark paint.

You're making progress.
Keep trying.

Oops, my potato burned!

Long finds a hidden place to practice . . . and practice . . . and practice some more.

He concentrates. He meditates.

He resorts to experimental methods.

He tries drinking hot tea . . .

eating spicy chili . . .

and letting the sun warm his belly.

But nothing works. Long only
spouts out warm, warm water.

"This is hopeless!" Long sighs.

At the end of the week, Professor McKay gathers the young dragons. "Are you ready for a picnic?" she asks.

Camila toasts marshmallows.

Willy pops popcorn.

Mia grills a fish.

Well done! Long, will you roast the pumpkin for us?

Long nibbles on his claws. His tummy feels tickly and squeezy. "Professor McKay, we won't have roasted pumpkin for our picnic. I'll let everyone down!" he cries. "Because where I come from, dragons breathe out water, not fire." Long's heart aches.

Professor McKay thinks for a moment. "I didn't know that.
We use water in cooking, too. Take it easy, and try your best!"

Long remembers what Professor McKay said:
find your own path.

He relaxes his body,
focuses his mind,
feels his power,
and . . .

A jet of hot, hot steam shoots out of his mouth.

But the pumpkin is not fire-roasted . . .

it is perfectly steamed.

When Long looks up,

the entire class is staring at him.

"Wow! When I breathe out water, it turns into hot steam!" Long smiles. "I found my unique talent!"

Together, the friends roast and steam, fill their bellies with delicious food, and have the most splendid picnic ever!

Long's adventure at Dragon School

has only just begun.

Author's Note

In this story, Long's name is based on the Chinese word for dragon, "龙 (lóng)." Like in Western culture, dragons are intricately intertwined with Chinese culture. However, Chinese dragons do not typically breathe fire. Instead, they are known as water spirits, and are believed to be the rulers of bodies of water, such as rivers and seas, and able to summon rainstorms.

As a first-generation immigrant who was born and raised in China, but has studied and worked in the U.S., I have always been fascinated by the differences and similarities between cultures. While living in America, I've realized that everyone is different and that learning from others helps you discover your own talents, while still allowing you to find your own path. My experience as a minority student in America inspired me to write this story. Dear reader, what is your goal? What is your talent and your path to achieving that goal? I can't wait to hear your stories.